SACRED Places of Kentucky

Photography by Wes & Stacey Battoclette
Written by Amanda Hervey & Rev. Roger Jasper

Foreword by Paul Prather

Published by Vested Interest Publications

SACRED

Places
of Kentucky

13-digit International Standard Book Number 978-1-934898-13-0
Library of Congress Card Catalog Number 2011913269

Design and production: Kelli Schreiber
Photography by Wes and Stacey Battoclette
Written by Amanda Hervey and Rev. Roger Jasper
Foreword: Paul Prather
Publisher: Vested Interest Publications

Manufactured in the United States of America

All book order correspondence should be addressed to:

Kentucky Monthly
P.O. Box 559
Frankfort, KY 40602-0559

1-888-329-0053
(502) 227-0053

www.kentuckymonthly.com

FOREWORD

By Paul Prather

I was born in Pulaski County and grew up primarily in Taylor County. During my boyhood, the religion I encountered was all Christian, nearly all evangelical ("You must be born again!"), and overwhelmingly Baptist.

That was partly because my dad was the pastor of a succession of rural Baptist churches, but it was also partly because evangelical Baptist Christianity predominated in the southeastern and south-central Kentucky of my youth.

Taylor County, for instance, had a population of roughly 20,000 back then, if memory serves me, yet supported several dozen Baptist churches and a four-year Baptist college. Almost everybody I knew was Baptist.

There's certainly nothing wrong with that. The point I'm trying to make is, until I was an adult, evangelical Baptist Christianity pretty much constituted all the religion I'd met.

It probably was not until in my 30s when I became the religion writer for the *Lexington Herald-Leader* that I realized Kentucky boasted a spiritual heritage as rich and diverse as any place on the planet.

My Baptist forebears were part of that history. Thousands of Baptists fled west during the late 1700s to escape sectarian violence in Virginia. They weren't the respected faith group they later became; they arrived here as a persecuted minority running for their lives, and they found sanctuary (in multiple meanings of that word) in Kentucky.

But the Baptists were only a piece of Kentucky's story. This state also was where the Second Great Awakening erupted. Among the more cataclysmic religious revivals on record, that movement began in Logan County and moved to Bourbon County. There, a meeting at Cane Ridge helped turn the South from a lawless frontier into the Bible Belt and birthed the Disciples of Christ, the independent Christian Church, and various branches of the Church of Christ.

Old Kentucky had loads of Methodists, Presbyterians, and Episcopalians, too. It was a hotbed of interdenominational wrangling.

Kentucky was where the Roman Catholic Church chose to establish its first United States diocese west of the Alleghenies, at Bardstown in 1808. Later, Trappist monks built a monastery not far from that town, the Abbey of Gethsemani, which eventually would become renowned worldwide as the home of Thomas Merton.

Indeed, the Commonwealth has played host to just about every manifestation of faith imaginable, from the sublime to the bizarre to the quaint: Quakers and Shakers and Jews and Edgar Cayce and snake-handlers and urban mega-churches and, more recently, Buddhists and Muslims and even a handful of Zoroastrians. You name them, they've discovered a home here.

Oddly enough, it was while visiting Texas a few years ago that I first saw a book like *Sacred Places of Kentucky*. In a shop there, I happened across a coffee-table book made up of photographs of various Lone Star houses of worship.

I thought it was a terrific piece of work. As I turned the pages, I said to my then-girlfriend (now my wife) Liz, "Somebody ought to do a book like that about Kentucky."

Fortunately, now somebody has. Stacey and Wes Battoclette have traveled across the Bluegrass photographing many of our most picturesque churches, large and small, famous and almost forgotten. Amanda Hervey and Rev. Roger Jasper have written the well-turned text that accompanies the photographs.

The finished project is lush, gorgeous, engaging, and frequently moving. In the following pages, you'll catch glimpses of sacred places I've already mentioned, including the Cane Ridge Meeting House and the Abbey of Gethsemani. You'll find others I'd never heard of, such as Snivley Chapel, a tiny Methodist church in Pike County, and Anshei Sfard, an Orthodox synagogue in Louisville.

Any given photograph might cause your spirit to soar.

Enjoy. Give thanks. Genuflect.

Paul Prather is pastor of Bethesda Church near Mount Sterling, Kentucky.

INTRODUCTION

By Amanda Hervey

While researching *Sacred Places of Kentucky*, I had the pleasure of talking with a 90-year-old woman who had spent nearly her whole life worshipping in the same place every week. As she spoke, I couldn't help but imagine those Sunday mornings. I pictured her grasping the white-gloved hand of her young daughter on Easter morning, envisioned her wiping joyful tears as her son passed her pew with his new bride on his arm, and felt the sting from a mental picture of a woman standing on legs weakened by time to honor the man she had married on that spot 60 years before his passing.

Sunday after Sunday, she had made her way to the same pew (three rows from the front on the right side) and each week dropped an offering into the passing plate. There were church picnics with her famous German potato salad (a recipe passed down from her great-aunt on her father's side), Vacation Bible Schools with popsicle-stick crosses pasted together and drying on cafeteria tables, and an ever-changing directory of members as people moved on, in one way or another. As the seasons of her life passed, she relied on her church to be the one steady thing in an ever-changing world—her rock. If anyone knew what made a place sacred, it would be this woman who had worn out the bottom of her shoes walking on hallowed ground.

When I asked her what it was that made her church sacred, she suddenly fell silent. "I don't have the authority to comment on that," she said. "I'm not a historian. I don't know enough about religion. I can't possibly define what is *sacred*."

She isn't alone in her uneasiness to define a word that seems too pure, *too righteous*, for us to grapple with our grubby fingers. This seems true of people of all denominations. We almost seem intimidated by the word, deeming ourselves unworthy of naming its meaning.

I know that is how I felt when I was asked to write this, a book that sets out to illuminate Kentucky's many sacred places. For me, the most sacred place I know in Kentucky is my grandpa's back yard, the place he called his church because that is where he felt closest to God. How could I possibly make a statement about what is sacred when my sacred place is under the shade of an oak tree?

But as I delved deeper into my research, I began to realize that the word "sacred" isn't at all white and pure as I had imagined. It is rugged, worn out and virtually used up. And best of all, it is a word covered in the fingerprints of seekers. You see, a place doesn't start out sacred. It isn't until the story is stretched over many generations, pulled so tightly in places that the fabric is tearing or worn thin enough to see through, that a place becomes sacred. Why? Because it is through those worn-out places that we see light.

Within the pages of this book, you will find a blend of places deemed sacred, representing a variety of denominations. From breathtaking feats of architecture to simple, one-room churches, this book attempts to illuminate the many ways Kentuckians define the word "sacred." As you note the differences in these places, I hope that you will see one key similarity among the featured places of worship: the seats, whether pews or chairs, all facing one direction. Though we pass each other on the streets and sometimes make brief eye contact in the frozen food section, our communities provide us little opportunity to be side by side, looking hopefully in the same direction. It is in these, our sacred places, that we come together. These places where we have gathered to celebrate, to pray, to worship and to live.

Calvary Episcopal Church, Ashland

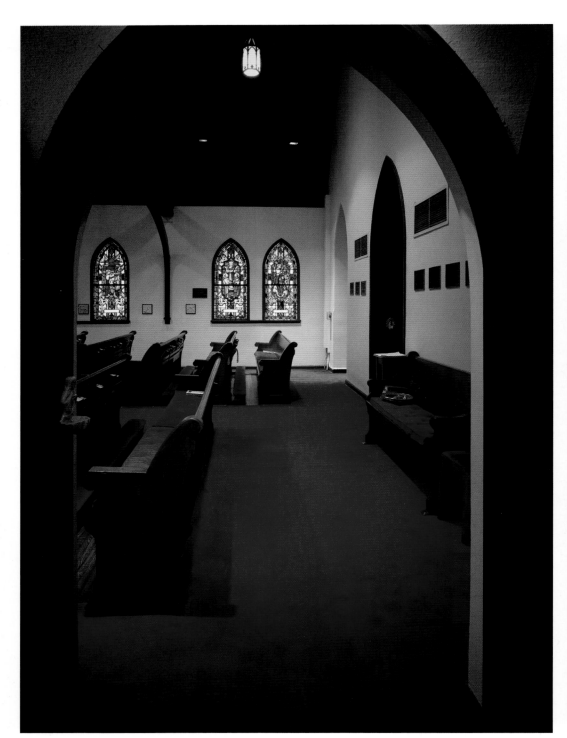

Calvary Episcopal Church, Ashland

Like those of many early Kentucky Episcopal churches, Calvary's beginnings were humble. Two years after a visit from the influential Bishop Benjamin Bosworth Smith in 1885, a formal Episcopal mission was established, and the first services were held in the minister's home. A year later, the cornerstone was laid for Calvary Church at 14th Street and Winchester Avenue, where the church still stands today. Three hundred worshippers gathered for its first service, which was held on Easter Sunday in 1889. Through three fires, 18 priests, eight bishops, and a constantly growing and changing congregation, Calvary has built a strong membership on that early foundation, with ready hands to serve its community.

1858 FIRST 1888
PRESBYTERIAN
CHURCH.

> *Remember the days of old, consider the years of many generations: ask thy father, and he will show thee; thy elders, and they will tell you.*

Deuteronomy 32:7

First Presbyterian Church, Ashland

"The history of a church is just such a remembrance ... Such history recounts the wisdom, insight, faith, and fidelity of our forebears. It reminds us that they found fundamental and rock-like things that put stability and permanence into people and communities. It reveals the richness of our heritage and the ground of our hope."

Passage taken from the introduction of A History of First Presbyterian Church *compiled by Mrs. D.F. Myers in 1954, which documented more than 130 years of the church's history, from its early roots as an open-air rural service to the 1950s.*

"He was moved with mercy."

Fathers of Mercy, Auburn

enciling that appears over the door at Fathers of Mercy, placed to remind
who enter that God dispenses His mercy freely within those chapel walls.

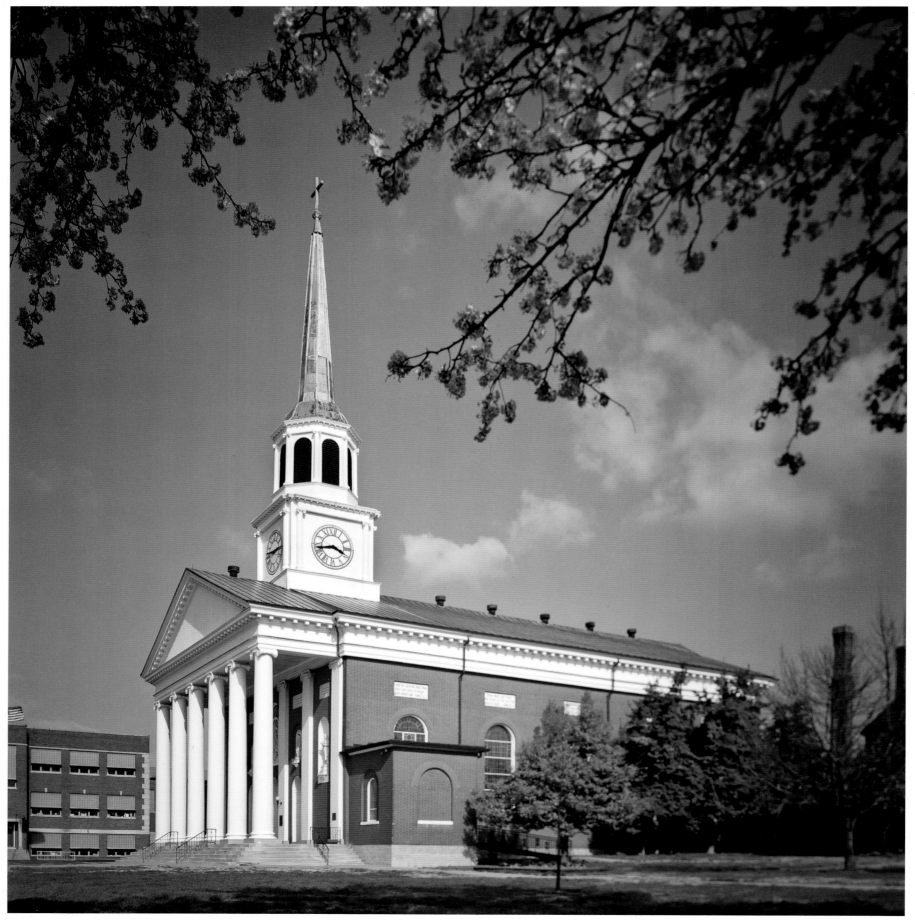

Basilica of Saint Joseph Proto-Cathedral, Bardstown

Until 1808, all of the Catholics in America were under a single diocese, Baltimore. On April 8 of that year, Pope Pius VII appointed a bishop to serve from New York, Boston, Philadelphia and Bardstown, Ky. The Basilica of Saint Joseph was built to be the seat of this bishop, whose pastoral responsibilities included the entire American frontier west of the Allegheny Mountains.

13

Saint Thomas Church, Bardstown

Built in 1816 a few miles south of Bardstown, this simple brick church served as the center of frontier Catholic life. The first seminary west of the Allegheny Mountains, the founders of the Sisters of Charity (an early orphanage), and the first bishop of the West were all hosted by this humble church.

"Herz Jesu"

Carved in stone above the entryway, this simple, German statement reminds all who enter to reflect on the heart of Jesus.

Sacred Heart (Divine Mercy Parish), Bellevue

By the late 1800s, a small town called Bellevue had sprung up on the Ohio River. Though a large majority of the population was Catholic of either German or Irish origins, there was no place for them to worship and celebrate their heritage. Most of Bellevue's Catholics walked to nearby Newport to attend Mass, but bad road conditions made the trip arduous. A small group of progressive members of the community gathered to organize what would become Bellevue's first parish. After many years in a temporary building constructed on two lots purchased in 1874, the congregation had witnessed a steady growth in membership and was able to move to its current location at the corner of Division Street and Taylor Avenue, which was dedicated on October 2, 1893. In recent years, Sacred Heart has combined with Saint Anthony Catholic Church to form Divine Mercy Parish.

16

Burton Memorial Baptist Church, Bowling Green

This congregation was founded as Drakes Creek Baptist Church in 1850 by Mordecai Ham. The name was changed when the grandson of founding member William Burton offered this unique stone sanctuary as a new home for the congregation in 1911. Ham's grandson and namesake was ordained at Drakes Creek. The younger Ham would go on to be a well-known evangelist and under his preaching Billy Graham would come to faith in Christ.

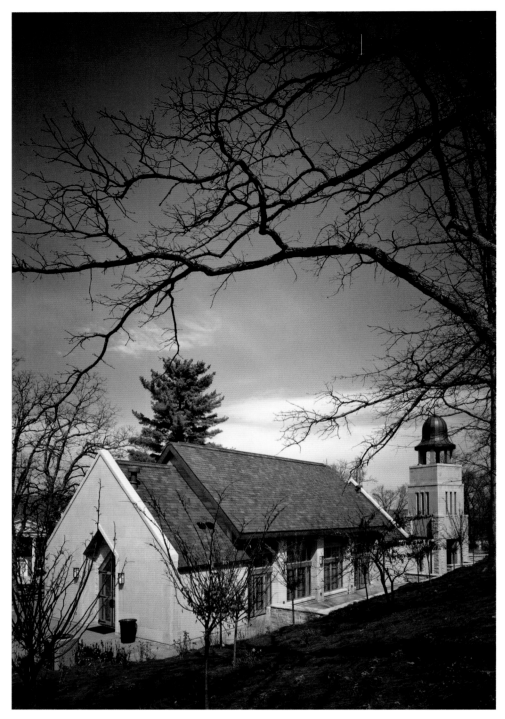

Chandler Memorial Chapel, Bowling Green

Dedicated on the campus of Western Kentucky University in April 2010 and made possible by the private support of WKU alumnus David Chandler and several benefactors, Chandler Memorial Chapel provides a sanctuary for students of all faiths. "The word 'jewel box' was used often to describe our vision for this building," said Helen Tyson Siewers, the landscape architect in the Planning, Design and Construction office at WKU who served on the planning committee for the chapel. "It was designed to be a small treasure, a place that let in light." One of the many unique features of Chandler Memorial, in addition to its etched-glass walls, is its columbarium. Derived from a Latin word that describes a place where doves nest, a columbarium provides a resting place for the remains of loved ones on sacred ground.

Chandler Memorial Chapel, Bowling Green

"*The spirit makes the Master.*"

— Dr. Henry Hardin Cherry, founder of
Western Kentucky University

Saint Joseph Catholic Church, Bowling Green

The construction of the Louisville and Nashville Railroad beginning in 1856 brought many German and Irish Catholic laborers to Bowling Green, which became a hub of activity at that time. Reverend Joseph DeBries, a native of Gerwen, Holland, was ordained and asked to organize a parish and build a church in Bowling Green to minister to the region's ever-growing Catholic flock. The congregation worshiped in a small temporary building until Francis Leopold Kister, a German master builder, began work on a brick building. Work was delayed due to the outbreak of the Civil War, but the building was completed in 1862. For more than 150 years, the members of Saint Joseph Catholic Church have built on that foundation to stand strong as a symbol of faith in our ever-evolving nation.

State Street Baptist Church, Bowling Green

In 1836, the slave members of First Baptist Church in Owensboro were permitted to begin having their own worship services. Two years later, they were dismissed to their own church. State Street Baptist, then First African and later First Colored Baptist, is the oldest predominantly black congregation in the area and one of the oldest in the state. This historic sanctuary dates back to 1873, and the Bible pictured is the church's original worship Bible. This church has twice been damaged by fire, but the congregation has persevered in faith.

The Presbyterian Church, Bowling Green

In 1833, famed architect Hugh Roland was on his way from Nashville to Louisville when he stopped in Bowling Green to draw plans for a new place of worship for Presbyterians in that region. They paid him $100. Some donated lumber, others gave stone and those who couldn't supply materials opened their purses. Little by little, the Presbyterian Church was built by the hands of its people. During the Civil War, occupying forces removed pews and windows, and in 1895, a fire nearly destroyed the steeple, but despite these and other setbacks in the church's more than 170-year history, the determination and faithfulness exhibited by those founding members exist today.

Mother of God Church, Covington

A handful of German Catholic families joined together 170 years ago to build a church where they could worship and celebrate the traditions of their Catholic heritage. It is Mother of God's focus on family that has made lifetime members of people like Victor Canfield, who follows in the footsteps of his grandparents and mother, who also were lifetime members. "Even in the midst of so much beautiful artwork, it is the simple things that I find to be sacred at Mother of God," said Canfield. "It's in that moment when I'm kneeling and the sun illuminates the face of a saint in the stained-glass windows that I had never noticed before, and I find myself reflecting on that saint's life and the light."

Mother of God Church, Covington

Saint Mary's Cathedral Basilica of the Assumption, Covington

Construction of Saint Mary's church began in 1894 after nearly a decade of planning was completed by Camillus Paul Maes, the third bishop of the Diocese of Covington. By 1915, funds were depleted and construction ceased, leaving the cathedral largely unfinished—when compared with Maes' vision—even today. In 1953, it was elevated to the rank of minor basilica by Pope Pius XII, an honor bestowed on only 35 churches throughout the United States. St. Mary's is home to one of the largest stained-glass windows in the world, measuring 67 feet tall and 24 feet wide. It is a monument to proclaim Mary as the Mother of God.

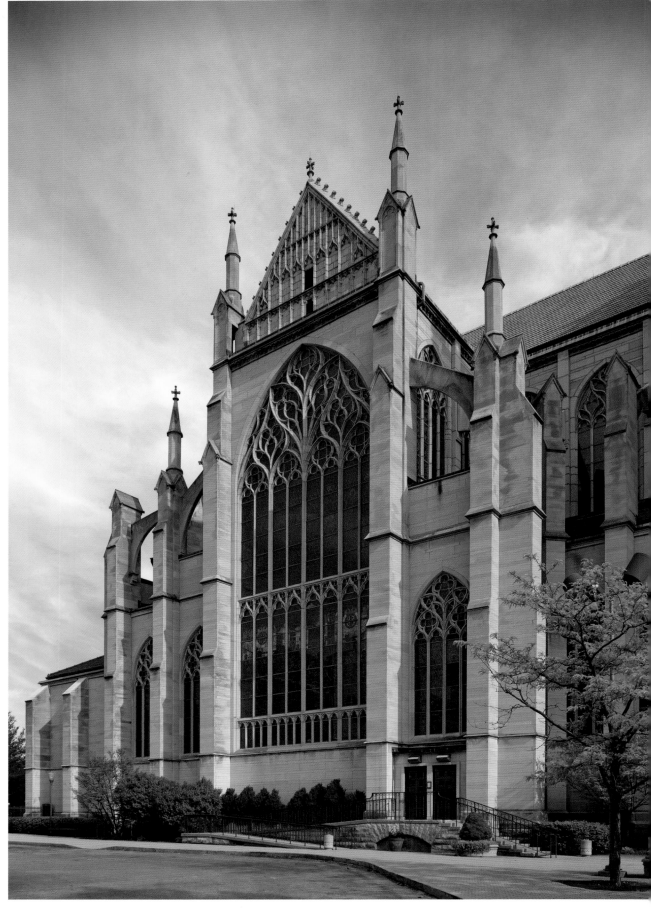

"To you, O God, I lift up my soul."

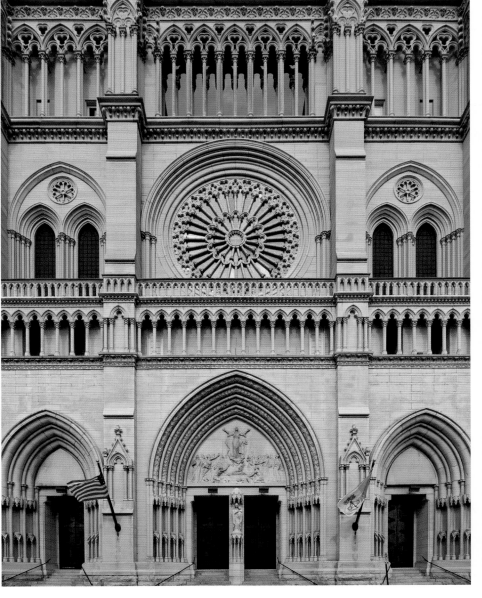

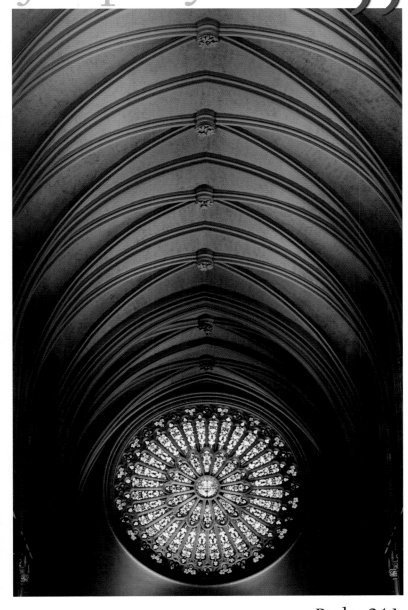

Psalm 24:1,
*as quoted in the Entrance Chant of the First Sunday
of Advent, setting the celebration of Mass in motion.*

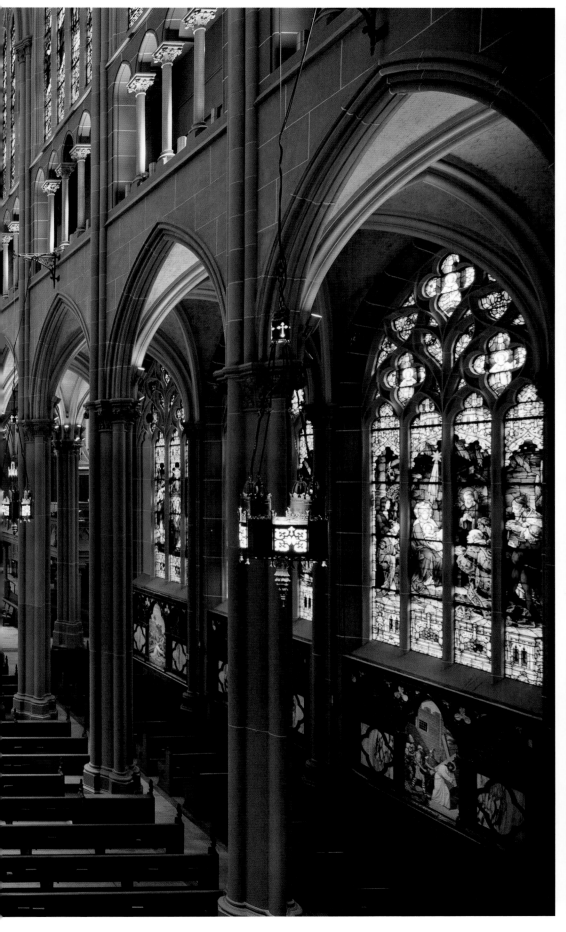

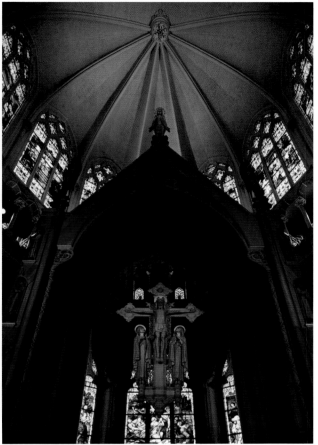

Christ Episcopal Church, Elizabethtown

More than 170 years ago, Reverend Benjamin Bosworth Smith, the first Episcopal bishop of Kentucky, visited Elizabethtown, where he was a guest in the household of A.H. Churchill, a prominent local judge. During his visit, Bishop Smith confirmed the judge and his family. Before that time, there was no Episcopal community in Elizabethtown, but that one visit set in motion more than a century of growth for that faith in the region. Between 1840 and 1850, Elizabethtown Episcopalians gathered where they could find space, be it in the homes of others or in borrowed churches, until Judge Churchill purchased land and built the present church. Though the members of Christ Episcopal Church have worshipped in that building since it was consecrated in April 1851, their humble beginnings are a reminder that it is the people who are the very heartbeat of this church body.

Church of the Ascension, Frankfort

When the congregation of the Church of the Ascension gathers on Sunday mornings, they worship where Christians of the Episcopal tradition have come together to praise God for more than 175 years. In 1835, the first Episcopal bishop of Kentucky, Benjamin Bosworth Smith, traveled to New York hoping to raise funds to build a seminary and churches in Kentucky. It was a gift of $1,000 from the ladies of the Church of the Ascension in Greenwich Village that was used to build a small, wooden frame church modeled after its benefactor church in New York. The church was named in honor of those women, who gave a gift nearly two centuries ago that continues to bless Kentuckians today.

Church of the Ascension, Frankfort

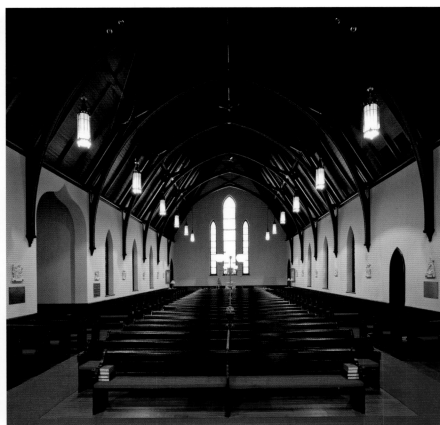

" *...Look with compassion on the whole human family; take away the arrogance and hatred which infect our hearts; break down the walls that separate us; unite us in bonds of love.* "

Prayer for the human family, taken from *The Book of Common Prayer* of the Episcopal Church.

Georgetown Baptist Church, Georgetown

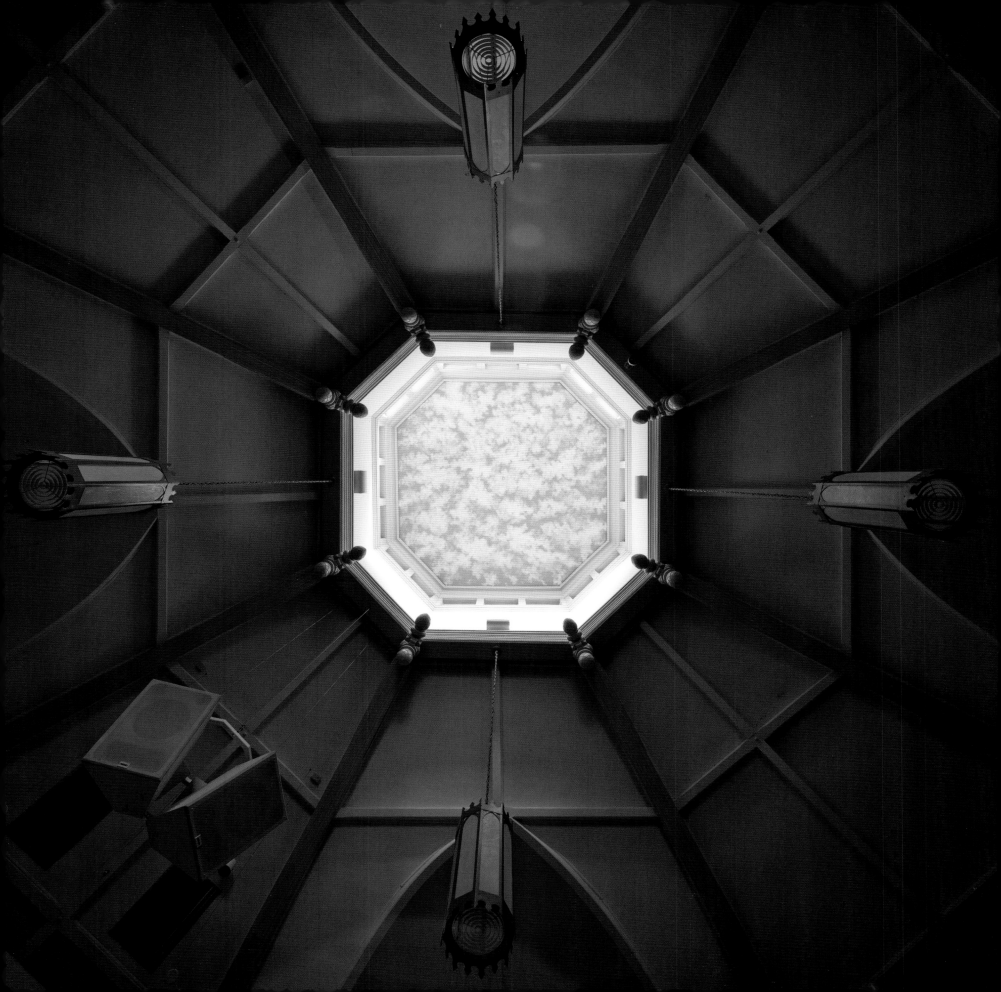

Georgetown Baptist Church, Georgetown

If the water was cold, I don't remember. What I do remember is the warmth of the sun shining through the stained-glass windows as the pastor lifted me out of the water into what felt like a new world and how my heart was so light and joyful, I nearly swam out of the baptismal.

Description of author Amanda Hervey's baptism at the historic Georgetown Baptist Church, which celebrated its 200th anniversary in September 2010.

ST. FRANCIS
MISSION

ESTABLISHED 1794

PRESENT CHURCH
ERECTED IN 1820

SECOND OLDEST
CATHOLIC CHURCH
WEST OF
THE ALLEGHENIES

Saint Francis de Sales Catholic Church, Georgetown

This church was initially pastored by Fr. Stephen Theodore Badin, the first person to be ordained to the Catholic priesthood in the United States. Saint Francis is the second-oldest parish in the state and the oldest in the Covington Diocese, and would emerge as the center for the Catholic mission to the eastern portion of Kentucky. From this rural spot in Scott County, four pastors would go on to be consecrated as bishops.

"Nothing is so strong as gentleness, nothing so gentle as real strength."

— Wisdom by Francis de Sales, namesake of the second-oldest church west of the Alleghenies.

Saint Francis de Sales Catholic Church, Georgetown

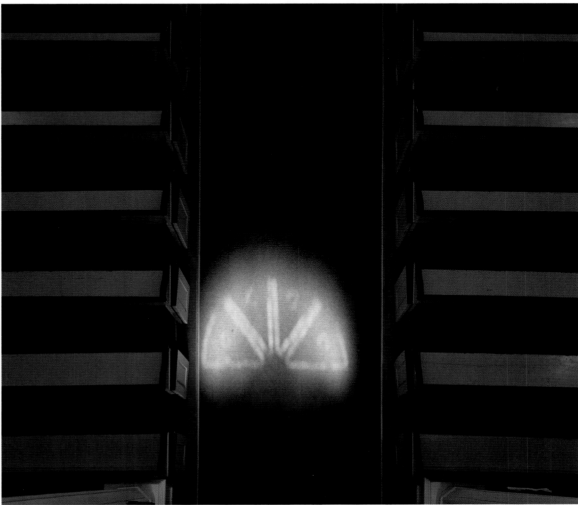

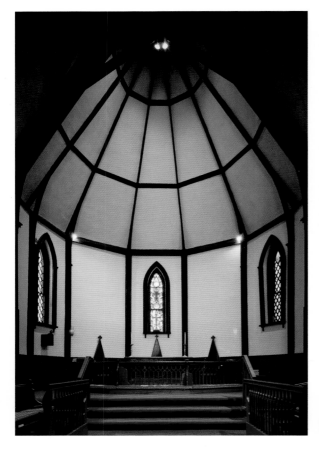

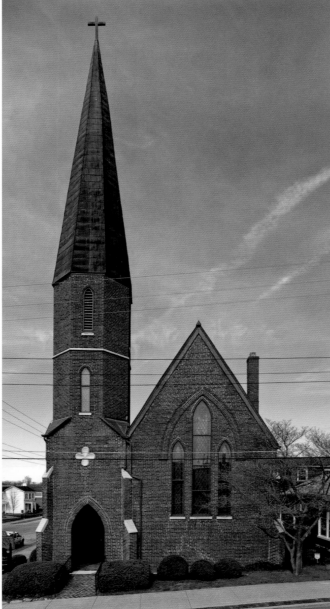

Saint Philip's Episcopal Church, **Harrodsburg**

Kentucky's first Episcopal bishop, Benjamin Boswell
Smith, was known to be a man of gentleness, kindness
and sincerity. He was commissioned to the difficult task
of pastoring a frontier state with very few Episcopal
churches. However, he was hands-on and personable with
clergy and laypeople around the state as he nurtured new
parishes into existence. The first worship service was held
at Saint Philip's on September 12, 1861. Bishop Smith not
only designed the church and supervised the construction,
but he carved the Communion altar himself.

Saint Augustine Church, Lebanon

Saint Augustine has a history of keeping priests for long tenures. The beloved Joseph Gettelfinger served the Lebanon parish for more than 30 years beginning in 1937. Father Gettelfinger was honored by Pope Pius XII with the title of Right Reverend Monsignor. He was known for being strict, but kind; one parishioner remembers him threatening during Mass to expel any of the parochial school students who attended an Elvis Presley concert. During the 1960s the local chamber of commerce recognized Monsignor Gettelfinger as citizen of the year for his leadership in the racial integration of local Catholic schools and parishes.

Saint Augustine Church, Lebanon

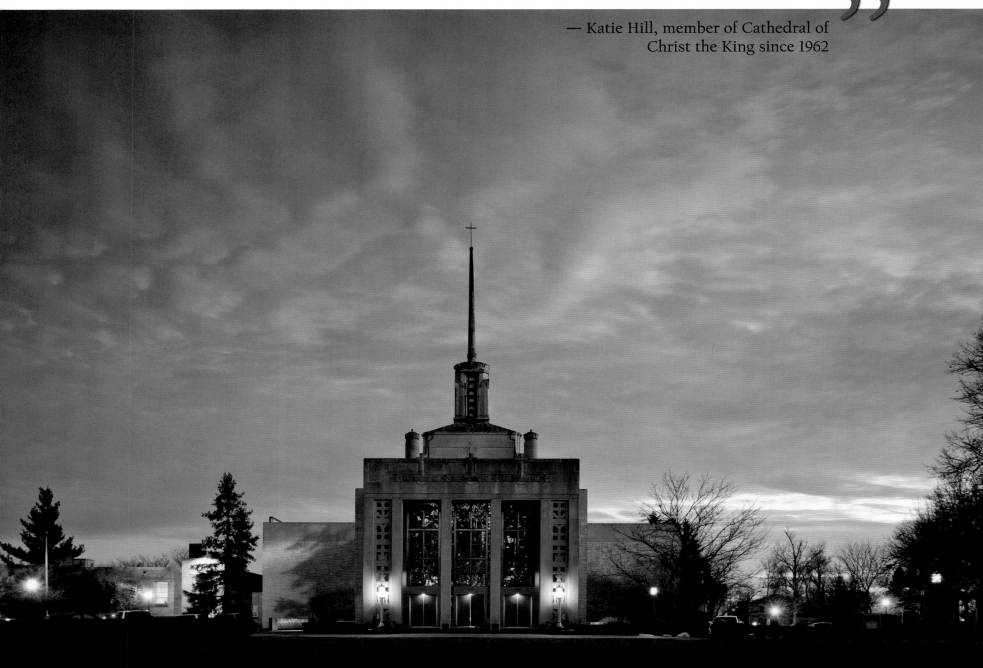

"It is where we met our friends, where we lived our lives. I had two children marry there and I buried my husband there. Those are the special moments, you know? The moments of a lifetime. I'll be there until they bury me, too."

— Katie Hill, member of Cathedral of Christ the King since 1962

Cathedral of Christ the King, **Lexington**

Cathedral of Christ the King, Lexington

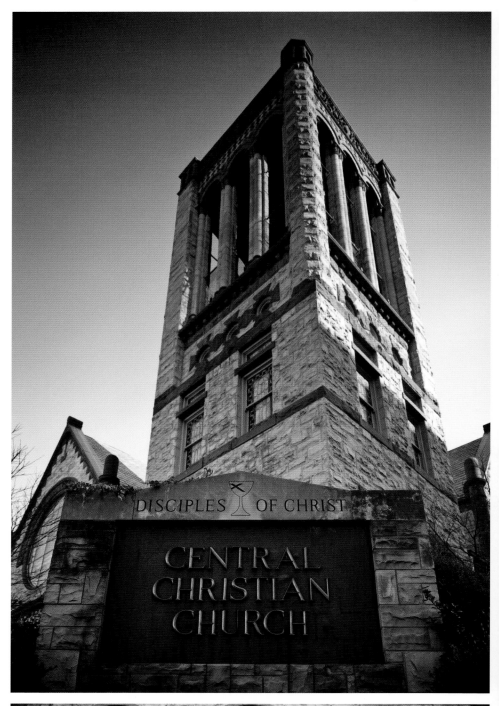

Central Christian Church, Lexington

In the revivals of the early 19th century, two movements for Christian unity emerged, one led by Alexander Campbell and one by Barton Stone. At Hill Street Church in Lexington, representatives met on January 1, 1832, to discuss merging the movements. At the meeting, "Raccoon" John Smith preached, "God has but one people on the earth. He has given to them but one Book and therein exhorts and commands them to be one family." After Smith's stirring sermon, union was marked by a handshake. Founded in 1816, Central Christian is the descendent of Hill Street. The current sanctuary dates to 1894.

"Come, let us sing for joy to the Lord; let us shout aloud to the Rock of our salvation. Let us come before him with thanksgiving and extol him with music and song."

Psalm 95: 1-2

Central Christian Church's music ministry is built on this Biblical foundation. In addition to the chancel, handbell and children's choirs, the church serves the Lexington community through its Central Music Academy, which provides music performance education to disadvantaged children.

Historic Pleasant Green Missionary Baptist Church, Lexington

The seed for the modern-day Pleasant Green Missionary Baptist Church was planted in 1790, when Peter "Brother Captain" Duerett organized the African Baptist Church. His small congregation met in a log church that his master, John Maxwell, helped him build at the convergence of Limestone and Euclid streets. The name was changed to Pleasant Green Baptist Church in 1829 so that slaves could easily identify it as a place of worship. After the passing of the beloved Brother Captain, the congregation came together to raise $850 to purchase the freedom of Reverend George W. Dupee, who led the church from 1855 to 1864. It was that spirit of giving and appreciation for the gift of freedom that brought Pleasant Green through some of the most trying racial issues in our nation's history and continues to propel the congregation in faithful service more than 200 years after its founding.

Temple Adath Israel, Lexington

The oldest Jewish congregation in Lexington, the Temple Adath Israel was founded in 1904 when a small group of Jewish men recognized the need to form a Reform Temple in the region to create a place of worship and celebration of the traditions of American Israelites. Those traditions and new ones are celebrated today, more than 100 years later, thanks to the support of Temple members like Susan Goldstein, who headed up a project to remodel the sanctuary. An artist herself, Goldstein became passionate about bringing the work of local artists into the Temple during its remodeling.

> *The presence of art in my place of worship is important to me because art is heavenly. Just as some respond physically to music, some respond to art. It is like a prayer.*
>
> — Susan Goldstein

Little Swiss Colony Church, London

With more and more Kentuckians moving west in the late 19th century, the Commonwealth began to extend an invitation to Europeans to immigrate to the Bluegrass. In 1881, a small group of Swiss immigrants found their way to Laurel County and formed a community named for Bern, Switzerland—Bernstadt—northeast of London. They came to work in the mines and built a life for themselves. In 1885, the community's first house of worship was built, the First Evangelical Reformed Church or Swiss Colony Church.

Twin Branch United Methodist Church, London

Feeling a need for a faith community to nurture their children, the people of the Twin Branch community in Laurel County organized the first church in the area in 1867, with their meeting house built in 1875. Rooted in the Methodist tradition, they have found inspiration in a motto known as "John Wesley's Rule." It reads:

Do all the good you can,
By all the means you can,
In all the ways you can,
In all the places you can,
At all the times you can,
To all the people you can,
As long as ever you can.

" *Go therefore and make disciples of all nations, baptizing them in the name of the Father and of the Son and of the Holy Spirit, and teaching them to obey everything that I have commanded you.* "

Matthew 28:19-20,
the foundation on which the United Methodist Church has been built

86

Holy Cross Church, Loretto

Having faced hostility and persecution in England, Roman Catholics in the New World found a safe haven in Maryland. In 1785, a group of Catholic families from Maryland set out over the mountains to settle on the frontier. They journeyed and settled together for mutual support and in the hopes that they would be able to call a priest. By 1787, they were celebrating Mass in their rustic homes. Soon after, this adventurous band would build Holy Cross, the first Catholic church west of the mountains, in Loretto. The current structure dates to 1823.

Congregation Anshei Sfard, Louisville

Congregation Anshei Sfard was incorporated in 1893 as the first Orthodox Jewish community in Louisville. The congregation met for holy days in borrowed spaces and had to leave its first permanent building to make way for interstate highway construction. The current synagogue was completed in 1955. Designed to facilitate adherence to the Torah, the facility includes a kosher kitchen, and the chapel is divided for men and women. The front of the synagogue features a beautiful stained-glass window of a menorah. Since the time of the tabernacle in the wilderness this seven-branched candelabra has been an important symbol in Jewish temples and synagogues.

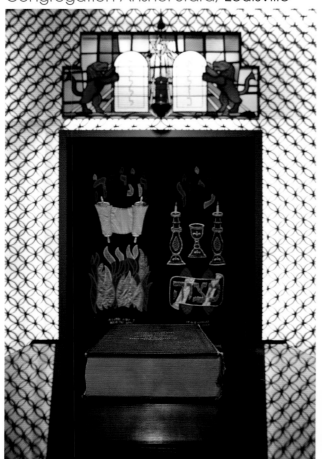

Calvary Episcopal Church, Louisville

Founded in December 1860, Calvary Episcopal Church was established when
the congregation of Sehon Chapel of the Methodist Episcopal Church seceded
from that denomination and joined the Episcopal Church. Members of that early
breakaway church continued to worship in the former Sehon Chapel through the
Civil War and following years. In 1872, the cornerstone was laid for a new building
at South 4th Street. The original front portion of that building still stands today
and includes the transepts and chancel areas. A stunning example of the Victorian
Gothic Revival style, Calvary Episcopal Church boasts a 70-foot-high arched ceiling
modeled after the famous hammer-beam roof of Westminster Hall in London.

Calvary Episcopal Church, Louisville

Cathedral of the Assumption, Louisville

After the diocese was moved from Bardstown to Louisville, the Cathedral of the Assumption was completed in 1858 and had, at that time, the tallest spire in North America. As we enter the Cathedral, we notice that the baptismal font is near the entrance. This illustrates how baptism serves to incorporate new believers into the Christian community.

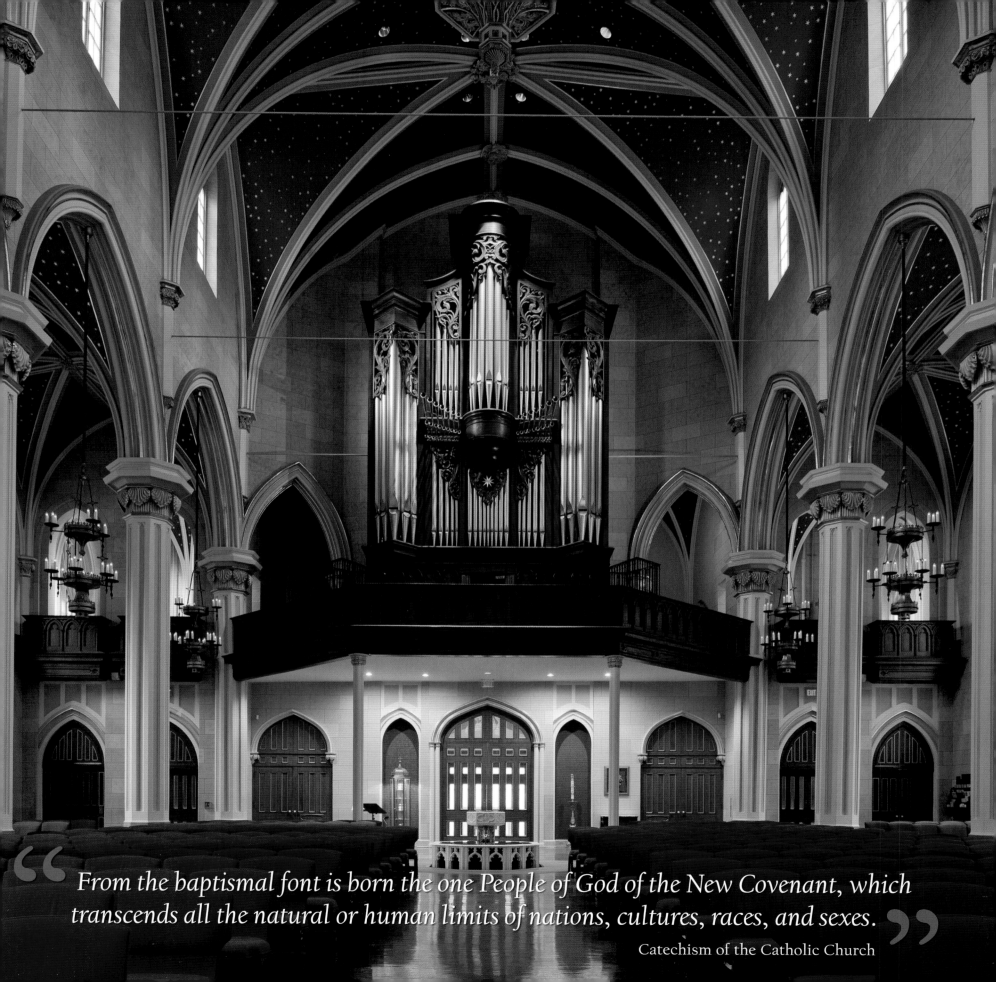

From the baptismal font is born the one People of God of the New Covenant, which transcends all the natural or human limits of nations, cultures, races, and sexes.

Catechism of the Catholic Church

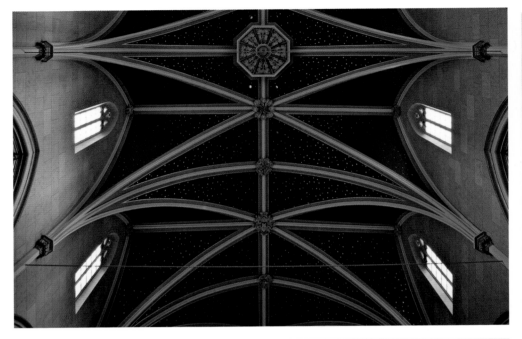

Cathedral of the Assumption, Louisville

First Lutheran Church, Louisville

Beginning with 14 members in 1872, First Lutheran has gone on to serve as the mother church to Lutheran congregations planted all across Louisville. Constructed in 1903, the current sanctuary narrowly escaped destruction under 1960s urban renewal. One of the most striking features of the sanctuary is the Last Supper wooden relief sculpture above the altar. This beautiful depiction of Jesus and his disciples was crafted by the early 20th-century artist Alois Lang. Lang learned the art of wood carving in Bavaria, where he was born and apprenticed at age 14. He is credited with the renewal of this medieval art.

Fourth Avenue United Methodist Church, Louisville

The area surrounding Saint Catherine and 4th streets has changed considerably since Fourth Avenue Methodist was chartered in 1888, but the congregation has stayed in Old Louisville and remained invested in Old Louisville. This church has a long and consistent history of diversity, cooperation and hands-on ministry to those most in need around them. The pews in the sanctuary are curved, so that every seat is facing the altar. The invitation is for all people to come and experience the love of God in Christ Jesus.

Our Lady of the Woods Chapel, Bellarmine University, Louisville

The Archdiocese of Louisville opened Bellarmine College in 1950. The chapel, which dedicated in 2001, hosts Catholic Mass, interfaith services and other events. The university was named for its patron, Saint Robert Bellarmine (1542–1621). Bellarmine was a university educator and theologian. He wrote, "The school of Christ is the school of love. On the last day, when general examination takes place, there will be no questions at all on the text of Aristotle, the aphorisms of Hippocrates, or the Paragraphs of Justinian. Love will be the whole syllabus."

Walnut Street Baptist Church, Louisville

In 1845, First Baptist (1815) and Second Baptist (1838) called the same pastor. The two congregations decided to merge and built a 600-seat sanctuary to accommodate the crowd. By 1902, still more space was needed, and Walnut Street built its current sanctuary. Walnut Street was one of the largest churches of its day. It has, however, followed a different route than many of the largest churches today. Instead of focusing on only building their own attendance, this congregation has taken a more cooperative approach and has participated in planting almost 80 other congregations around Louisville.

First Christian Church, Mayfield

As followers of the Stone-Campbell movement settled in Mayfield, there was need to organize a Christian church. After meeting in homes and public buildings, a small church was built in 1868, and the current building was constructed in 1908. First Christian's sanctuary is crowned with a magnificent dome supported by an octagon. During 1996 renovations, the monochromatic paint of recent years was replaced with vibrant colors closer to the 1908 originals. In the color is meaning. The blue of the dome envisions the heavenly realm. The royal purple of the octagon reminds the worshiper that Christ is mediator between heaven and earth.

Saint Mary's Episcopal Church, Middlesboro

Like many early Episcopal churches throughout Kentucky, St. Mary's emerged from humble beginnings. In the late 1800s, Anglicans and Episcopalians in the Middlesboro region gathered to worship at the Colgan Print Shop, in the lobby of the Middlesboro Hotel or in a borrowed Baptist church. Money was subscribed to support the organization of a mission, and the Town & Lands Company provided the lot where the church stands today. St. Mary's was formally dedicated in February 1891. Today, it is considered to be one of the finest representations of Carpenter Gothic architecture in the nation.

Third Baptist Church, Owensboro

Third Baptist Church began the 20th century as the largest and most famous Baptist congregation in the Commonwealth, meeting in the most spacious sanctuary in the South. Its distinctive mission and no-holds-barred character so captured the imagination of guest evangelist J. Frank Norris that he returned to Texas to build the biggest church in the country and become the most flamboyant preacher in the nation. Norris would come to be known as one of the most controversial figures in Southern Fundamentalism. A century later, the church motto is "Christ first, others second, we're Third."

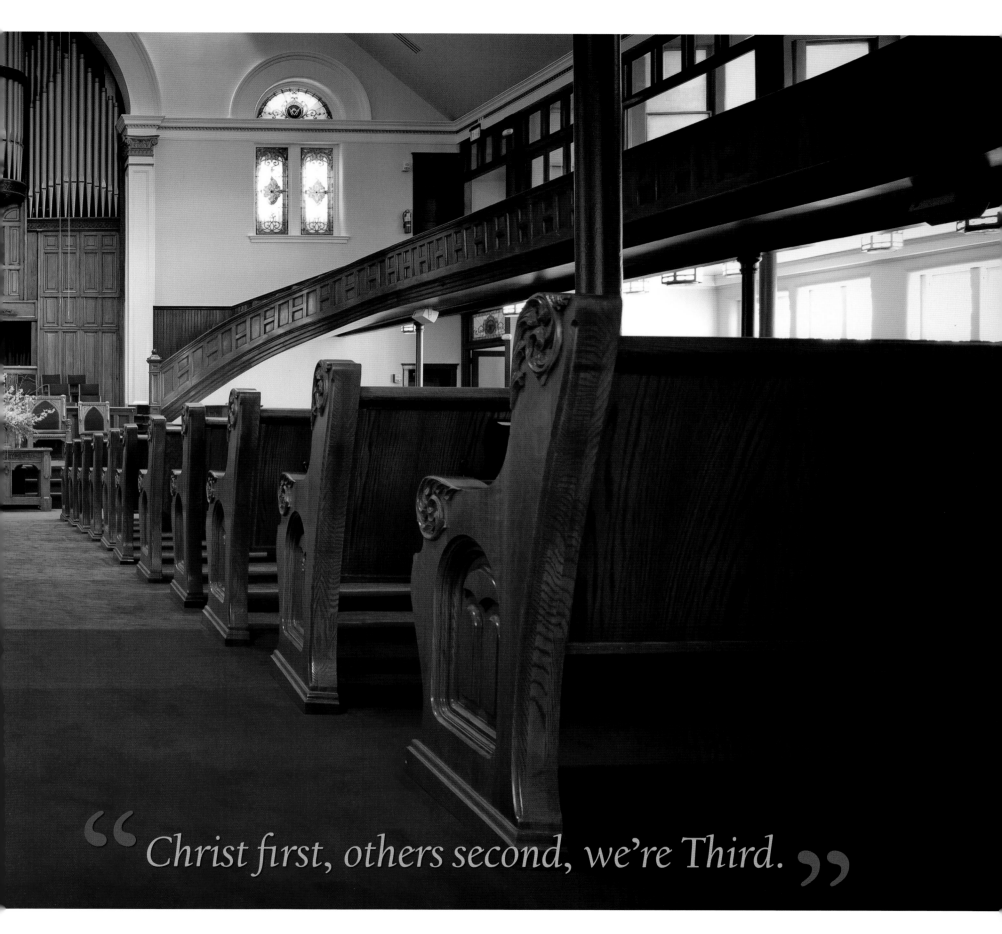

"*Christ first, others second, we're Third.*"

Grace Episcopal Church, Paducah

During the very early years of Grace Episcopal Church, members gathered in private homes and in the McCracken County Courthouse to conduct services. By 1851, the resolute congregation had its first church building, which was located between Washington and Clark streets. During the Civil War, that building was used as a makeshift hospital for federal troops. After those traumatic years, the members broke ground on a new and larger church building. Though work was slowed by a cholera epidemic in the summer of 1873, enough progress had been made to hold the first services there the following summer. Harriet Bowell, a witness to that first service, wrote that the incomplete building had "... old pews bearing the marks of the army mules' teeth, no plaster on the walls, no ceiling overhead, no glass in the windows." Determination to gather in faithful worship brought the members of that church through some of the most difficult times in our nation's history. Today, the church members have embraced the "tree of life" as their symbol to remind them that, like their rich history, faith grows from a seed into a mighty tree.

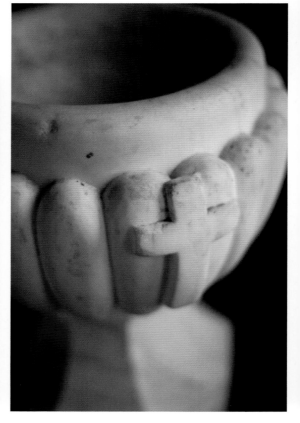

Saint Francis de Sales Catholic Church, Paducah

The first Catholic church built in Paducah, Saint Francis de Sales has a rich history that began in 1848 when well-known missionary priest Elisha Durbin formed the church. Land at Sixth and Broadway was purchased for $225 that same year. After more than 160 years and several new constructions and renovations to accommodate the ever-growing congregation, Saint Francis de Sales remains the only church in Paducah to stand on its original property.

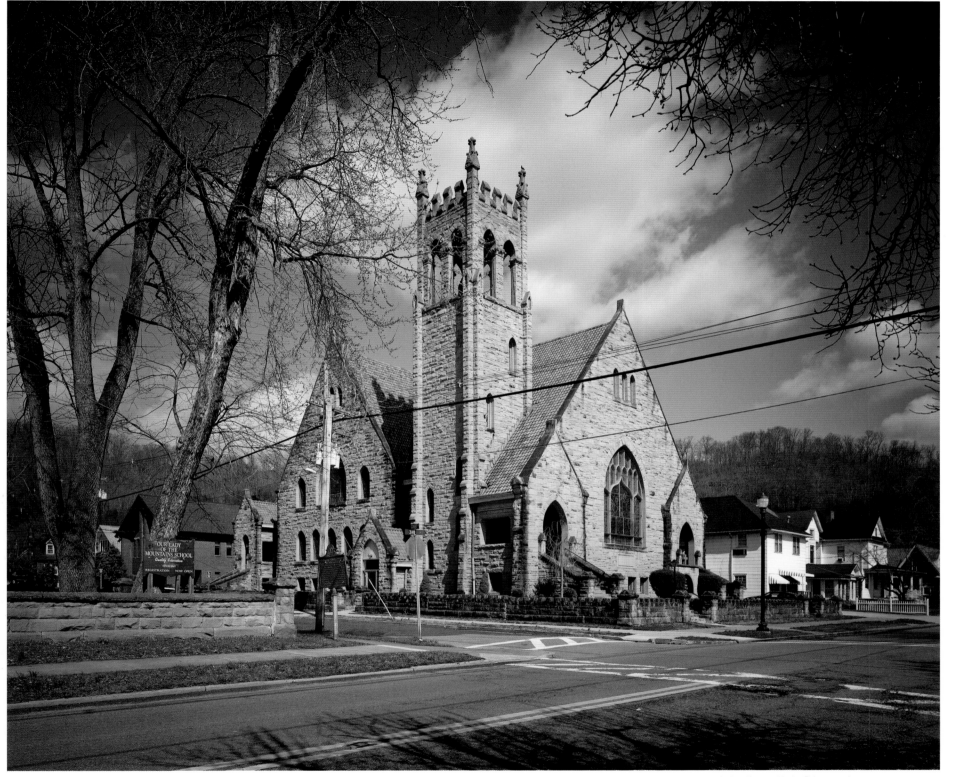

Mayo Memorial United Methodist Church, Paintsville

Built in 1904 by wealthy educator and entrepreneur John C.C. Mayo, Mayo United Memorial Methodist is a stunning representation of a church built in the Gothic Revival style. The building was constructed of native sandstone transported by a tramway and sculpted on site, and the stones were laid by 100 Italian stonemasons. The pointed arches, one of the church's distinguishing features, eliminated the need for steel for window and door lintels and are symbolic of praying hands. The organ, built by the Pilcher Organ Company of Louisville, was donated by Andrew Carnegie in 1910.

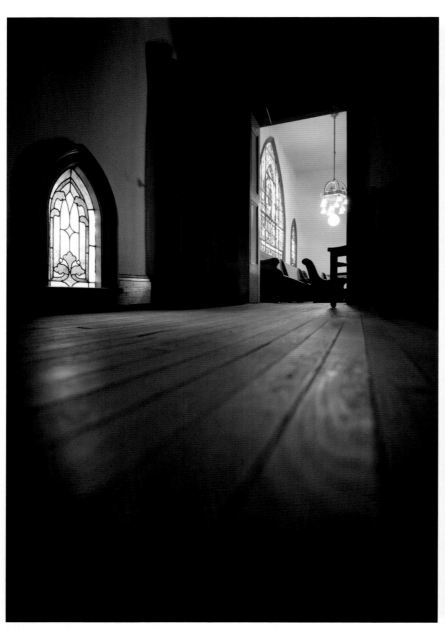

Mayo Memorial United Methodist Church, Paintsville

"Though we cannot think alike, may we not love alike? May we not be of one heart, though we not of one opinion?"

— John Wesley, founder of the Methodist Church

Cane Ridge Meeting House, Paris

One of the most significant events in the history of religion in America took place in August 1801 when Bourbon County Cane Ridge Church, pastored by Barton Stone, hosted an ecumenical revival. As many as 30,000 people attended. Extraordinary demonstrations of zeal and emotion were witnessed, such as fainting and barking. This enthusiasm spread from Cane Ridge across the country and led to the Second Great Awakening. Stone would became a leader in a new movement for Christian unity. Christian Churches and Churches of Christ can trace their origins to this ridge outside of Paris.

130

Snivley Chapel, Pikeville

Built on land deeded by the Leslie family in 1853, Snivley Chapel was constructed on John's Creek that year with poplar wood cut on the creek's nearby steam-powered sawmill. Snivley was the first Methodist meeting house in Pike County and has served as mother to many others in the county. The chapel is named for Rev. W.J. Snivley, an early Methodist circuit rider in the area. The circuit riders were ministers who would preach at several rural gatherings and would ride on horseback many miles to teach and care for the dispersed believers.

ENROLLMENT

ATTENDANCE
LAST SUNDAY

OFFERING
LAST SUNDAY

ATTENDANCE
TODAY

OFFERING
TODAY

Built of poplar wood harvested from the forests of Pike County, Snivley Chapel stands as a memorial to those early Kentuckians who believed this soil to be hallowed ground and laid a foundation on which generations could build.

Pikeville United Methodist Church, Pikeville

"They devoted themselves to the apostles' teaching and to fellowship, to the breaking of bread and to prayer. Everyone was filled with awe at the many wonders and signs performed by the apostles. All the believers were together and had everything in common. They sold property and possessions to give to anyone who had need. Every day they continued to meet together in the temple courts. They broke bread in their homes and ate together with glad and sincere hearts, praising God and enjoying the favor of all the people. And the Lord added to their number daily those who were being saved."
Acts 2:42-47 (NIV Translation)

Scripture held sacred by the congregation of Pikeville United Methodist, who have gathered since 1912 in their church located on Pikeville's historic Huffman Avenue.

Abbey of Gethsemani, Trappist

On a cold December day in 1848, 44 Cistercian monks from the Abbey of Melleray in Brittany, France, arrived in Nelson County. In rustic cabins, they began the daily practices of work and prayer that have continued nonstop since that time. Eight times each day they gather together to chant Psalms and pray for the life of the world. Here at Gethsemani is where Kentucky's most famous 20th-century spiritual writer, Thomas Merton, spent most of his life.

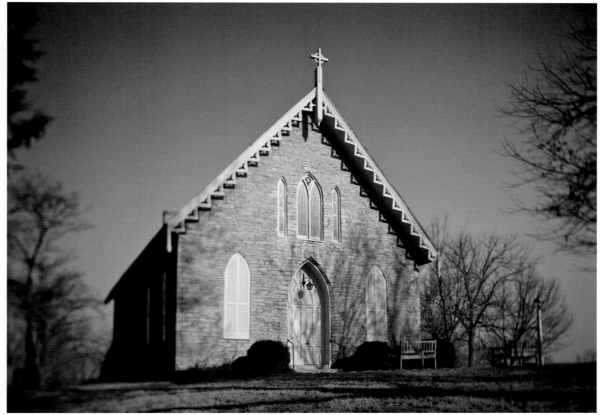

Pisgah Presbyterian Church, Versailles

"What makes Pisgah Presbyterian Church hallowed ground? Its people. For 227 years, the people of Woodford County and beyond have gathered on this ground to marry their sweethearts, baptize their children, raise their families and bury their loved ones. They have sustained this ground through times of great trial and tribulation and have celebrated here in times of triumph. The history of this great church does not lend itself to a museumesque atmosphere but rather enlivens us with the knowledge that God has been active in this place for generations and will be for generations to come. Yes, this is certainly a sacred place."

— Rev. Pete Jones

“ *God is currently and personally present in*
the wilderness, in the garden and in the field. ”
— Martin Luther

KENTUCKY MAP

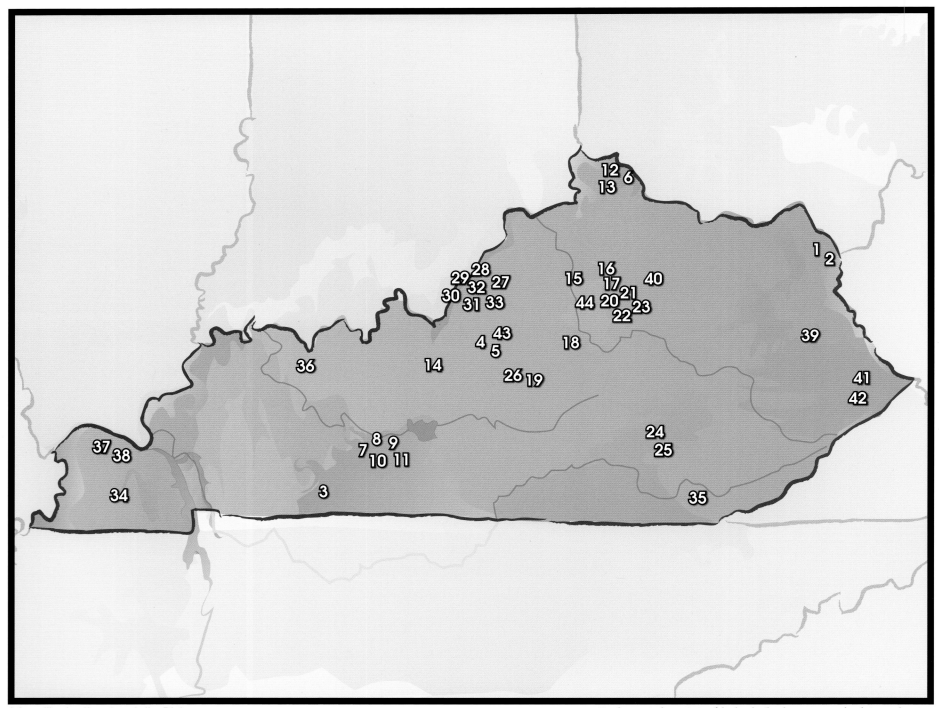

Map illustration by Julie Ridge

Numbers are in the proximity of the churches, but do not correspond to their exact locations.

INDEX

FROM THE PHOTOGRAPHERS
By Wes & Stacey Battoclette

When you think of a sacred place, a lot comes to mind. For us, a sacred place can be a grand cathedral or even a small white chapel that sits on a winding country road miles from any city. But it is not those buildings alone that make it sacred; it is the people, their objects, their beliefs, their acts of worship, and their community that fill those spaces, breathing into them life and meaning.

Driving down the rolling hills just outside of Lexington toward our first church for this book, we had no clue what to expect or where this journey and experience would take us. As we pulled into the parking lot at Saint Francis de Sales that afternoon under a rare cloudless blue sky in the dead of winter, we knew this was going to be a great start to what would become *Sacred Places of Kentucky*. And it was—the light that poured into the sanctuary that day not only inspired us but guided us to places that we may otherwise have overlooked. During the two hours we were there, we saw the light

slowly sweep from one side of the sanctuary to the other, making the space, although empty, come alive. We could feel the history and the life in the sanctuary that afternoon, and that experience is what laid the foundation for the rest of this book.

There were many times during the creation of this book that we had the opportunity to photograph during a service. A very memorable church for us was the Historic Pleasant Green Baptist Church in Lexington. We attended a Sunday morning service at this church, and to say the people there were friendly would be an understatement. They were so welcoming, loving, and happy to have us there. We captured their hearts in times of prayer, giving, and worship. Another experience that will be unforgettable is the chance happening when we arrived at Saint Joseph Catholic Church in Bowling Green just as a service was beginning during Catholic schools week. All the children were participating in the service and watching intently as Fr. Andrew placed the Eucharist into the tabernacle. This was a sacred moment that we were thrilled to be a part of. Saint Joseph has such a grand history that has been very well preserved, which made capturing the details within the sanctuary and the sacristy exciting.

The wide range of sacred places in Kentucky is astonishing. One of the most unique of those for us was the Abbey of Gethsemani, a Trappist monk society in the heart of Kentucky. What caught our attention was their sanctuary, which is very minimal in its design. We learned from one of the monks that it was designed that way to allow fewer distractions during times of worship and prayer. This not only served an important purpose, but it allowed for striking images, especially during an afternoon prayer service. Hearing the organ come to life and the monks sing out not only brought a sense of completion to the space but seemed to magnify it.

Every place we visited had a story, told through the people, acts of worship, sacred objects, and architecture. Together, all of these places and so many more tell the story of the rich history and beauty that make up the *Sacred Places of Kentucky*.

This book has been an amazing experience and adventure for us. We would like to thank all the participating churches for graciously opening their doors and sharing their sacred places with us. We will never forget all the wonderful people we met and the many stories they shared.

ACKNOWLEDGMENTS

By Amanda Hervey

I've heard it said that a church is like a body, and each member has a role in moving the body forward. The head provides the leadership, the hands ready themselves for the task, the arms bear the weight and the legs keep the body steady. No one body part is more important than the others because without support, it wouldn't function to its fullest potential. This simple image of the church as a body, though a Christian metaphor, describes so well the role sacred places hold in our communities and also the creative process we've experienced in documenting those places throughout the Commonwealth.

The publishing of *Sacred Places of Kentucky* can be credited to *Kentucky Monthly*'s director of marketing, Kendall Carr Shelton. Just as the word "head" cannot convey the significance of that body part's role, her title fails to express the profound way she has served the company for more than 10 years. Decisive, confident and capable of finding a way around any and all roadblocks, Kendall's leadership has made this project possible when snow, bad hotel rooms, budget crunches and impossible deadlines made it seem anything but. She took an idea cooked up by an often-dreamy editorial staff and made it a reality.

When it came time to select the "eyes" for this project, we couldn't think of a better pair than husband-and-wife duo Wes and Stacey Battoclette. They have taken a "what-if?" idea we pitched them over cold pizza and have given us the opportunity to view the world as they do, with optimism and an impeccable talent for finding light when the rest of us find only darkness. For three months, they packed their lives up with their gear and overnight bags to travel to the far corners of the Commonwealth in an effort to give sight to our fuzzy vision. You will find that each photograph featured in these pages is a testament that the eyes really are the window to the soul.

Kelli Schreiber, *Kentucky Monthly*'s art director, deserves praise as the "hands" of this creative body. With an uncompromising work ethic and ability beyond her years, Kelli has taken the raw parts brought together by the rest of us to weave together the compilation you now hold. As you explore the pages of this book, you may not notice the presence of her work because it is so seamless and subtle, but I assure you, her fingerprints are all over it.

I must thank my dear friend, Roger Jasper, senior minister at Living Faith Baptist Fellowship in Elizabethtown, for being the "other foot." His passion for Kentucky's religious history, contagious energy and tireless research brought balance to the writing of this book. It is our hope that Roger's ability to convey historical significance and my enthusiasm for telling the "heart stories" blend together before you to illuminate what makes these places sacred without leaning too heavily in one direction.

As the author of the Kentucky A to Z series, I have had the pleasure of traveling all sorts of Kentucky roads to seek out stories hiding somewhere between Main Street and the hollers. No matter where I am, be it ritzy or rural, nearly abandoned or buzzing with activity, places of worship are always at the heart of the community, and you will find that is the case with this book. Our goal was not to define the word "sacred" because, as it is with traveling, there is always more than one road to travel, but we do make an effort to share with you the postcards of a heart-journey we've been fortunate enough to embark on through our great state. We did not consider religion when choosing the sacred places to feature but instead focused on architecture, history and story, and rather than tell you about those things, we set out to show you. After all, isn't it more powerful to feel a heart beat than have someone describe it?

I want to thank others who have propelled this creative body. Steve and Kay Vest, thank you for seeing three competent and steady professionals where the world may see three frazzled, coffee-driven and overly ambitious mommas. Your faith in our often off-the-wall ideas is more appreciated than you'll ever know. A special thanks to Patricia Ranft, who spent many hours booking hotel rooms for the photography team and poring over our copy that was prone to late-night errors. Lindsey McKinney, thank you for your tremendous marketing efforts to get this book into the hands of our readers and beyond. Thanks to Madelynn Coldiron and Ted Sloan for their copy editing prowess. And to every hand this book has passed through during its printing, distribution, display and review, we are grateful for the role you've had in bringing *Sacred Places of Kentucky* to fruition.

Last but not least, we would like to thank the leadership and members of the featured sacred places. Thank you for sharing your spaces, your stories and your lives. Your role, no matter how big or small, strengthens not only your place of worship but also your community. You are the heartbeat of this book and of this Commonwealth, and without you, we are moving forward with nowhere to go.